PRAYERS
FOR MY
FUTURE HUBBY

GABRIELLE HARRIS

Copyright © 2023 Gabrielle Harris All rights reserved. No part of this publication may be reproduced, distributed, or transmitted in any form or by any means including photocopy, recording or other electronic or mechanical
methods without prior written permission of the author Gabrielle Harris.

ISBN: 979-88518330-4-5
First Edition July 2023. Printed in the United States of America.
Published by: www.heavenscallingllc.com

Table of Contents

Allow Him to Be Himself	6
Trust Him	7
Believe Him	8
Believe in Him	9
See the Best in Him	11
Be a Peacemaker	12
Work Together	13
Remember, He's Not My Enemy	15
Put Forth Effort	17
Fight for Him	19
Be Productive	21
Be Flexible	23
Know What I Want	25
Know Your Values	27
Respect Him	29
Have Healthy Boundaries	31
Respect Yourself	33
Be Loyal	35
Have Fun	37
Compromise	39
Give Him Time	41
Submit	42
Allow Him To Lead	44
Take an Interest in His Interests	46
Don't Neglect	48
Compliment	50

Table of Contents

Create Safe Space	52
Stay Focused on God	54
Remember All the Things You Like About Him	55
Encourage	57
Support	59
Love Him	60
Plan Date Nights	62
Tell Him You Love Him	64
Forgive Easily	66
Give Grace	68
Give Space	70
Compassion	72
Be Content	74
Let God Change Him	76
Appreciate Him	78
Listen to Him	79
Be Patient	81
Nice New Clothes	83
Pray for Him	86
Be Classy	89
Show Him You Love Him	90
Be Open	92
Fix My Hair to Look Nice	94
Be Positive	96
Take Care of Me	97

Allow Him to Be Himself

Dear Lord Jesus,

    I pray I will allow my future hubby to be himself. I pray I won't try to change him but allow you to change him, mold him, and shape him to be the person you've called him to be before the beginning of time. I pray he will walk in his calling and be committed to the call, purpose, and plans you have for his life. I pray his heart will remain open to you and that he will remain loyal to you. In the name of Jesus Christ,

    Amen.

Trust Him

Dear Lord Jesus,

    I pray I will trust my future hubby. I pray I will be able to trust him to lead properly and effectively. I pray I will be able to trust him with my heart. I pray he will create a safe space for me to trust him. I pray I won't try to control him or worry about the things I can not control with him; I pray I will give you all the fears, worries, and concerns that I have about him and our marriage. In the name of Jesus Christ,

    Amen.

Believe Him

Dear Lord Jesus,

    I pray I will believe my future hubby. I pray that I believe his words and his actions. I pray he is an honest man with integrity and one who can be trusted. I pray he keeps his word and aims to do what he says he will do. In the name of Jesus Christ,

    Amen.

Believe in Him

Dear Lord Jesus,

    I pray I will believe in my future hubby. I pray that I will support him. I pray I will always see the best in him. I pray I will always encourage him to do better and be better. I pray there is never a day that goes by that I'm not speaking life to him, in every dead area and place of his life. I pray he will feel alive. I pray he will feel inspired and motivated. I pray he will be strengthened. I pray he will be empowered to go out here and do all you've called him to do and be all you want him to be in the name of Jesus Christ. I pray I will always see his highest potential and encourage and push him to reach his highest potential, all for your kingdom, glory, and purpose, Lord Jesus, in

(continued)   *Believe in Him*

the name of Jesus Christ. I pray when he is feeling down; he will read your Holy Word (the Bible), listen to inspirational Christian music, and pray and seek your face like never before, in the name of Jesus Christ. I pray you will renew his strength and that he will wait on you, mount up with wings as eagles, run, and not be weary, and walk and not faint, in the name of Jesus Christ. I pray the joy of the Lord will be his strength. I pray he will endure to the end. I pray he will run the race to reach the finish line with you, Lord Jesus. When it is time to leave this Earth, I pray that you will say, "Well done, my good and faithful servant," in the name of Jesus Christ. Hallelujah! Glory to God. You're awesome, Lord Jesus. Worthy, worthy is the Lamb of God who was slain for the sins of the world. Glory, glory, glory, glory. Thank you, Jesus. In the name of Jesus Christ,

Amen.

See the Best in Him

Dear Lord Jesus,

    I pray I will always see the best in my future hubby. I pray I will see the best in his character. I pray I will see the best in his work and ministry. I pray I will see the best in his friendships. I pray I will see the best in his family. I pray I will see the best in our marriage. I pray I will see the best in his fatherly duties. I pray I will see the best in his spousal duties. I pray I will see the best in all the roles he plays. I pray I will always see the best efforts that he puts forward. In the name of Jesus Christ,

    Amen.

Be a Peacemaker

Dear Lord Jesus,

    I pray I will be a peacemaker with my future hubby. I pray I will create peace in our marriage. I pray I will create peace in our conversations. I pray I will create peace in the decisions I make and the actions I take. I pray I will create peace in our home. I pray I will always strive to create peace between me and my future hubby. I pray you will bless me for creating peace in our home and relationship. In the name of Jesus Christ,

    Amen.

.

Work Together

Dear Lord Jesus,

    I pray my future hubby, and I will work together as a team and that it will be a team effort. I pray we will always work well together. I pray we will work well together in our finances. I pray we will work well together in our businesses. I pray we will work well together in our ministry. I pray we will work well together on household chores. I pray we will work well together in planning events and parties. I pray we will work well in studying, learning, and growing together. I pray we will work well together in our giving of time, energy, and effort. I pray we will always get along well with each other so we can do all and be all you have called us to be before the beginning of time. In the name of Jesus Christ. Let our yest

(continued)   **Work Together**

for each other be yes. Let our no for each other be no. Let our maybes for each other be a maybe and thoroughly considered. Let us be realistic with each other and not expect more than what we can actually give. Let us show grace to each other and be merciful. Let us strive to put each other's needs, wants, and desires before our own. Let us strive to make each other a top priority in the name of Jesus Christ. I pray we will work together out of our love for you, Lord Jesus, and our love for each other. I pray we will have the same goals and work together on implementing those goals in our marriage, kids' lives, ministry, businesses, friendships, family, and other areas of our life, in the name of Jesus Christ. With you at the center of our marriage Lord Jesus, I know we can work well together with your help. In the name of Jesus Christ,

    Amen.

Remember, He's Not My Enemy

Dear Lord Jesus,

    I pray I will remember my future hubby is not my enemy. I pray I will never treat him like an enemy. I pray I will know when the enemy is moving and speaking through him and that I won't bow down to the enemy. I pray I'll submit to God, resist the devil, and he will flee. I pray I will rebuke the enemy and command him to leave every time I see him show up in our home, our conversations, and our marriage. I pray I will stay in prayer for my future hubby. I pray I will earnestly pray for him and continually cover him in prayer, day and night. I pray I will put on the whole armor of God, so I will be able to stand firm against all strategies of the enemy in the name of Jesus Christ. I thank you, Lord Jesus, that my

(continued) # Remember, He's Not My Enemy

future hubby and I are victorious in you, and with your help, we will defeat the goliath that tries to rise up in our marriage and family life in the name of Jesus Christ. Goliaths do fall, and giants do fall, in the name of Jesus Christ. No weapon formed against our marriage will be able to prosper. In the name of Jesus Christ,

    Amen. Amen. Amen.

.

Put Forth Effort

Dear Lord Jesus,

    I pray my future hubby, and I will put forth effort in our marriage and family. I pray we will never give up, and when we feel like we're at our breaking point, you will give us strength to fight, stand, and endure in the name of Jesus Christ. I pray we won't be weary in doing well in our marriage, for in due season, we shall reap if we faint not. I pray many treasures and blessings will be stored up for us in Heaven. These treasures are rewards for us doing well, putting forth effort in our marriage, and helping each other to fulfill the call of God over our lives in the name of Jesus Christ. Thank you, Jesus, for strength. Thank you,

(continued)   Put Forth Effort

Lord Jesus, for helping us to put forth the effort in our marriage. In the name of Jesus Christ,

    Amen.

Fight for Him

Dear Lord Jesus,

    I pray I will fight for my future hubby when he feels like giving up, is discouraged, is burdened by the cares of this world, or feels he can't take any more pressure. I pray I will stand and fight for him. I pray when he feels like his good is not enough and when he's tried all options he thinks are possible, that I will stand and fight for him. When he feels hopeless and has no hope, I pray I will stand and fight for him. When he feels unloved and unappreciated, I pray I will stand and fight for him. When he's almost at the end of it, I pray I will stand and fight for him. When he doesn't see the end, I pray I will stand and fight for him. When his dreams are crushed, I pray I will stand and fight for him. When perfection and even at his

(continued)   Fight for Him

best is not enough, I pray I will stand and fight for him in the name of Jesus Christ. I pray I will stand and fight for him in prayer. I pray I will stand and fight for him through support. I pray I will stand and fight for him with words of encouragement. I pray that you will show me ways to stand and fight for him in the name of Jesus Christ. I pray I will not give up and throw in the tower but stand and fight for him and our marriage. In the mighty name of Jesus Christ,

    Amen. Amen. Amen.

Be Productive

Dear Lord Jesus,

I pray my future hubby, and I will be productive together. I pray we will be productive together in business and ministry. I pray we will be productive together in our marriage. I pray we will be productive together in our family. I pray we will be productive in all we do together. I pray we will be productive in our communication to date night planning or spending quality time with each other. We live for you, Lord Jesus, and I pray we keep you at the center of our marriage. I pray a day does not go by that we're not being productive in our marriage and putting you first. May we always be productive in loving each other and serving each other in love. I pray our marriage

(continued)   Be Productive

is so productive that, as a married couple, we're producing an abundance of fruit for you, and the work we do for your kingdom, glory, and purpose shall be rewarded. In the name of Jesus Christ,

    Amen.

.

Be Flexible

Dear Lord Jesus,

    I pray I will be flexible with my future hubby. I pray I will be willing to compromise and go with the flow when plans change, and unexpected things come up. I pray I will be flexible with my future hubby's time and flexible when he's tired or not in the mood. I pray I will be flexible out of love for him. I pray I will be flexible out of patience for him. I pray I will be flexible out of understanding for him. I pray I will constantly be flexible out of appreciation for my future hubby. Thank you, Lord Jesus, for helping me to be flexible with my future hubby in the name of Jesus Christ. I thank you, Lord Jesus, that I can do all things through you, and you give me the strength to be flexible in your name. I pray flexibility will

(continued)   Be Flexible

come naturally and easily to me. I pray for a more understanding, compassionate, and empathetic heart for my future hubby. I pray for a greater measure of love, so being flexible is easy. I pray that he will appreciate my flexibility and love me and not take advantage of my gentle, quiet spirit, understanding heart, and flexible mindset. I pray he will value it and show his appreciation for my being flexible for him in the name of Jesus Christ. I know with your help, Lord Jesus, I can be flexible, and so can my future hubby. In the name of Jesus Christ, I pray our flexibility for each other will help our marriage to grow, and I pray you will use it for our good. Thank you, Lord Jesus. In the name of Jesus Christ,

    Amen.

Know What I Want

Dear Lord Jesus,

    I pray I will know what I want with my future hubby. I pray it won't take me a long time to make decisions. I pray I will make wise and thoughtful decisions quickly and effectively. I pray I will be content, happy, and satisfied with what I want and going after it. I pray I will be committed to my future hubby and always want him and always want to be married to him. I pray I will never be unwavering in my decision to marry him, stay married to him, and be with him. I pray he knows my heart, my love for him, and my loyalty to him and our marriage. I pray he never has doubts in his mind about what I want. I pray he will be confident in knowing that it is him that I want and that being with him is pleasing you,

(continued) # Know What I Want

Lord Jesus. You put us together for the purpose of assignments and ministry in the name of Jesus Christ. I pray I'll still want my future hubby when times get tough, when tests and trials come, in the name of Jesus Christ. I pray I will still want my hubby when we agree to disagree. I pray I will still want my hubby when I see his imperfections as a man and mortal being. I pray I will love every part of him and make allowance for his faults, show mercy, and show grace to him. In the name of Jesus Christ,

    Amen.

Know Your Values

Dear Lord Jesus,

    I pray I will keep my values with my future hubby. I pray I will value myself and not lower my standards for him or anyone else. I pray I will value our marriage and our friendship. I pray I will value my ministry and businesses. I pray I will value my body. I pray I will value you, Lord Jesus, by spending time with you in the wee hours of the morning, putting you first, and keeping you first in my heart. I pray I will value Heaven more than this Earth and store treasures in Heaven. I pray I will value living out your will here on Earth and staying in your will (living out the purpose and plans you have for my life). I pray I will value the Promise Land and all the blessings you have for me. I pray I will value loving my neighbor as (continued)   Know Your Values

myself and loving you, Lord Jesus, with all my heart, mind, spirit, and soul, in the name of Jesus Christ. I pray I will value you, Lord Jesus, more than anything, and because I cherish you, I pray I will value my future hubby and loving people. I pray I will eternally value you, my hubby, kiddos, family, and loving people, in the name of Jesus Christ. I pray I will value, love, respect, and honor myself in the decisions I make, the actions I take, and all that I do. In the name of Jesus Christ,

    Amen.

Respect Him

Dear Lord Jesus,

    I pray I will respect my future hubby. I pray I will respect him in the actions I take, the decision I make, and the words I use. I pray I will respect him in how I communicate with him. I pray I will respect him in how I love him and show my love for him. I pray I will respect him by including him in all decisions and allowing him to share his input and lead. I pray I will respect him as a leader. I pray I will respect him as a hubby. I pray I will respect him as a father. I pray I will respect him in ministry and business. I pray I will respect him in his work. I pray I will respect him with his time. I pray I will always respect him and (continued)   Respect Him

that he knows that I respect him. Thank you, Lord Jesus, for helping me respect my future hubby. In the name of Jesus Christ,

    Amen.

Have Healthy Boundaries

Dear Lord Jesus,

    I pray I will have healthy boundaries with my future hubby. I pray I won't overstep but honor those boundaries we have for each other. I pray I will give him appropriate space when he needs it. I pray for healthy boundaries so we will have a healthy relationship. I pray you will show me how to have healthy boundaries with my future hubby so we can have a successful and healthy marriage and continue to minister together for you, help upbuild your kingdom, help win souls for you, and do all you've called us to do. I pray that with the love and support of each other and healthy boundaries, all will be possible for your kingdom, glory, and purpose. Lord, help me to see the

(continued) # Have Healthy Boundaries

importance of healthy boundaries in our marriage and with your kids, family, and friends. In the name of Jesus Christ,

    Amen.

Respect Yourself

Dear Lord Jesus,

    I pray I will respect myself in my future marriage with my future hubby. I pray I will respect myself, my time, my commitments, and my loyalties. I pray I won't put more demands on myself than I can bear. I pray that I will take time for myself. I pray I will practice self-care and self-love by pampering myself. I pray I will make decisions out of respect for myself. I pray I will do and say things out of respect and love for myself. I pray I won't love myself less because I'm married or expect my partner to love me more. I pray I will create a positive atmosphere by first respecting myself and respecting others in the name of Jesus Christ. Please show me ways to

(continued)

Respect Yourself

respect and love myself more. Thank you, Lord Jesus. In the name of Jesus Christ,

    Amen.

Be Loyal

Dear Lord Jesus,

    I pray I will be loyal to my future hubby. I pray I will always be loyal to him, no matter what. Through all the tests and trials, I pray I will stay loyal to him. I pray I will stay loyal to him in my actions and words. I pray I will stay loyal and committed to him always. I pray I will stay loyal to our marriage and keep our marriage bed holy. I pray I will stay loyal to loving him and serving him in love. I pray I will stay loyal in being a loving and supportive wife. I pray I will stay loyal to him by being the best wife and woman I can be. I pray I will stay loyal to him by remaining loyal to God and my holy commitment to stick by my hubby and love him til death do us part. I pray you will help me and show me how always to be loyal to

(continued)   Be Loyal

my future hubby, Lord Jesus. In the name of Jesus Christ,

    Amen.

Have Fun

Dear Lord Jesus,

    I pray my future hubby, and I will have fun together. I pray we will find ways to have fun and make the marriage fun together. I pray, from the smallest to the biggest things, that we will have so much fun together. I pray that we will be happy in everything that happens in our day. I pray you will show us how to have fun in our marriage, on date nights, in our day-to-day activities, and with one another. I pray that you will keep the marriage alive, well, and healthy with the help of fun ideas and lots of joy in the name of Jesus Christ. I pray my future hubby and I will be open to fun on trips, fun at home, fun at work, fun with ministry and businesses, fun at church, and fun with whatever *(continued)*   *Have Fun*

we do. Thank you, Lord Jesus, for fun experiences and a fun marriage. In the name of Jesus Christ,

    Amen.

Compromise

Dear Lord Jesus,

    I pray I will compromise with my future hubby and always compromise with him. I pray it'll be easy for me to compromise with him on decisions. I pray it will be easy for me to compromise with him on fun. I pray it will be easy for me to compromise with him on vacations and trips. I pray it will be easy for me to compromise with him on food places. I pray it will be easy for me to compromise with him on date nights. I pray it will be so easy and that my hubby will love me for it. I pray it will be easy for me to compromise with him on our present and future plans. I pray you will help me, Lord Jesus, to compromise with my future hubby in the name of Jesus (continued) *Compromise*

Christ. Please show me ways we can compromise together. In the name of Jesus Christ,

    Amen.

Give Him Time

Dear Lord Jesus,

    I pray I will give my future hubby time. I pray I will give him time for his shortcomings, mistakes, and slip-ups. I pray I will give him time if he's busy. I pray I will give him time when he's tired. I pray I will give him time when he needs alone time. I pray I will give him time when with his friends and family. Out of love for him, I pray I will give him time whenever and however he needs it, in the name of Jesus Christ. I pray you will help me to give my hubby time. In the name of Jesus Christ,

    Amen.

Submit

Dear Lord Jesus,

    I pray I will submit to my future hubby. I pray that it'll be easy for me to submit to him. I pray I will submit to him as my hubby, the father of our future kiddos, and the man and leader of the house. I pray I will submit to his leadership and allow him to lead. I pray I will submit to his plans for us and our marriage. I pray I will submit to his plans for our kids and family. I pray I will submit to his goals for us and himself. I pray I will submit to him as we are one body and one in your eyes, Lord Jesus, in the name of Jesus Christ. I pray I will submit to his guidance. I pray I will submit to him as a wife who submits to her hubby.

(continued) *Submit*

I pray you will show me how to submit to my future hubby and honor him through submission. Thank you, Lord Jesus, for helping me to submit to my future hubby. In the name of Jesus Christ,

    Amen.

Allow Him To Lead

Dear Lord Jesus,

I pray I will allow my future hubby to lead me. I pray I will allow him to be the leader of our home. I pray I will respect him as the leader. I pray I will honor him as the leader. I pray that he will lead with confidence, boldness, and bravery. I pray he will lead with instructions from you. I pray he will lead with guidance from you. I pray he will lead while being submissive to you. I pray he will lead with a heart that is one hundred percent surrendered to you, Lord Jesus. I pray he will lead by being guided by your Holy Spirit and not by the flesh. I pray he will lead by following your Holy Word and his convictions. I pray he will lead by

(continued)

Allow Him To Lead

listening to your voice. I pray he will be the leader you want him to be and call him to be, all for your kingdom, glory, and purpose. In the name of Jesus Christ,

    Amen.

Take an Interest in His Interests

Dear Lord Jesus,

    I pray I will take an interest in my future hubby's interests. I pray I will be open to exploring new experiences and adventures with him. I pray I will keep an open mind to his interests, likes, and hobbies. I pray I will take an interest in his pleasures. I pray I will take an interest in his friends and the people he likes to spend his time with. I pray I will take an interest in what he likes to eat. I pray I will take an interest in the tv shows and movies he likes to watch. I pray I will take an interest in the songs he likes to listen to. I pray I will take an interest in the vacay places he likes to explore. I pray I will take an interest in what he likes to do for *(continued)* # Take an Interest in His Interests

fun. I pray I will take an interest in what he likes for relaxation. I pray I will take an interest in what he likes to do for dates. I pray I will always take an interest in who he is and the core of who he is. I pray I will take an interest in the things that bother him and make him sad, upset, and worried. As a wife, I pray I will take an interest in his desires, wants, and needs in marriage. I pray there is never a day that goes by that I don't take an interest in my future hubby. Thank you, Lord Jesus, for helping me to take an interest in my future hubby's interests. In the name of Jesus Christ,

    Amen.

Don't Neglect

Dear Lord Jesus,

    I pray I will not neglect my future hubby. I pray I will attend to his needs, wants, and desires. I pray I will honor his needs, wants, and desires. I pray I will spend quality time with him. I pray I will give him everything that will help him. I pray I will provide him with everything a godly wife gives her hubby. I pray he always feels like his needs, wants, and desires are addressed. I pray you will show me ways to adhere to his needs, wants, desires, and passions. I pray you will help me to support him when he needs support. I pray you will help me to love him when he doesn't feel love. I pray you will help me do everything I need to ensure his needs are met in the marriage and his *(continued)*   *Don't Neglect*

life. Thank you, Lord Jesus, in the name of Jesus Christ. Please help me to make sure his physical needs are met. Please help me to make sure his emotional needs are met. Please help me to make sure his spiritual needs are met. Please help me to make sure his relational and social needs are met. Please help me ensure his educational and learning needs are met. Help me, Lord Jesus, so my hubby never feels neglected but always feels cared for and loved. With your help, Lord Jesus, I can be the supportive, compassionate, caring, and empathetic wife you need me to be. In the name of Jesus Christ,

    Amen.

Compliment

Dear Lord Jesus,

    I pray I will compliment my future hubby. I pray I will compliment him on his entire outfit. I pray I will compliment him on his appearance. I pray I will compliment him on his character when he does well. I pray I will compliment him on his actions and good choices. I pray I will compliment him on his work ethic. I pray I will compliment him on his ministry and accomplishments. I pray I will compliment him on his skills, abilities, and creativity. I pray I will compliment him on his efforts. I pray I will compliment him on his meals and food choices. I pray I will compliment him on his work around the house. I pray I will compliment him on fulfilling my needs, desires, *(continued)*   *Compliment*

and wants. I pray I will compliment him on everything and every opportunity I have. I pray I will compliment him so he feels appreciated and good about himself and his various roles as a hubby, father, worker, ministry worker, and child of God. All for your kingdom, glory, and purpose. In the name of Jesus Christ,

    Amen.

Create Safe Space

Dear Lord Jesus,

    I pray I will create a safe space for my future hubby. I pray I will create a safe space for him to learn and grow. I pray I will create a safe space for him to express his feelings. I pray I will create a safe space for him to share his wants, needs, and desires. I pray I will create a safe space for him to be open and honest. I pray I will create a safe space for him to open his heart to love me. I pray I will create a safe space for him to be vulnerable with me. I pray I will create a safe space for him to do what he wants. I pray I will create a safe space for him to care for himself and love himself. I pray I will create a safe space for him to spend time with his family *(continued)*   *Create Safe Space*

and friends. I pray I will create a safe space for him to do what interests him and what he loves doing the most. I pray I will create a safe space for him to be himself. I pray I will create a safe space for him to relax and have peace and quiet. I pray I will create a safe space for him to have alone time. I pray I will create a safe space for him to be independent and have his own thoughts and opinions. I pray I will create a safe space for my future hubby so he will always want to come home to me and always be married to me. I pray I will create a safe space for him so we can have a successful marriage. I pray you will help me to create a safe space for my future hubby. Thank you in advance, Lord Jesus, for your help. In the name of Jesus Christ,

    Amen.

Stay Focused on God

Dear Lord Jesus,

    I pray I will stay focused on you when I am married. I pray I will not get distracted by the cares of this world but rather put you at the center and keep you at the center of my life and my mind so that I can be the best me in my marriage. I pray I will stay focused on you in all the different seasons of marriage. I pray I will stay focused on you in my free time, spare time, and chill time with my future hubby. I pray I will stay focused on you, Lord Jesus, during date nights with my hubby. Pray I will stay focused on you and always be intentional with focusing on you, Lord Jesus. In the name of Jesus Christ,

    Amen.

Remember All the Things You Like About Him

Dear Lord Jesus,

    I pray I will remember everything I like about my future hubby. I pray I'll focus on the things I love about him and make him uniquely him. I pray I will remember all the things I like about my future hubby to help show love to him and help encourage him when he feels discouraged. I pray I'll remember to help motivate him when he's lacking motivation and to help support him and build him up by painting out all the great things about him. To show gratitude and appreciation, I pray I will remember everything I like about my future hubby. I pray I will remember everything I like about my future hubby, never *(continued)* # Remember All the Things You Like About Him

forget and focus on those things all the time. With your help, Lord Jesus, I know you can help me to remember all the things I like about my future hubby. Thank you, Lord Jesus, for allowing me to remember all of the things I like about my future hubby. Thank you, Lord Jesus. In the name of Jesus Christ,

Amen.

Encourage

Dear Lord Jesus,

    I pray you will help me to encourage my future hubby when he's feeling discouraged. I pray you will help me to encourage my hubby when he's tired, feeling weak, and worn out. Pray you will help me to encourage my future hubby when he's weary and on the verge of giving up and throwing in the tower. I pray you will give me the words to speak life to him in the name of Jesus Christ. I pray you give me the words to speak hope to him in the name of Jesus Christ. Pray you give me the words to speak courage to him in the name of Jesus Christ. Pray you will give me the words to speak strength to him. Pray you give me the words to speak words of encouragement to *(continued)*   *Encourage*

him, in the name of Jesus Christ. May my words always uplift him and help him for his now and future, in the name of Jesus Christ. I pray when he's down, my words will encourage him, he'll feel like a load was lifted, and he'll have the desire to keep going, pressing, and enduring. In the name of Jesus Christ. Thank you, Lord Jesus, for helping me to encourage my future hubby and showing me the ways. In the name of Jesus Christ. Thank you, Lord Jesus.

    Amen. Amen. Amen.

Support

Dear Lord Jesus,

    I pray I will support my future hubby. I pray I will support him in ministry, work, and family. I pray I will support him in relationships and friendships. I pray I will support him in his various roles. I pray you will always help me to support my future hubby in the name of Jess Christ. I pray he will never have to question whether or not I support him. I pray it will always be apparent that I am highly supportive of him. In the name of Jesus Christ,

    Amen.

Love Him

Dear Lord Jesus,

    Please help me to love my future hubby to the fullest and unconditionally. Please show me ways to show him love without idolizing him. Please show me how to love him properly without worshipping him. Please show me how to deny myself, pick up my cross, and love him. Please help me to love him the way you love him, Lord Jesus. Please help me love him without limitations, conditions, or prerequisites. As you freely love me, I pray I will freely love him, in the name of Jesus Christ. I know with your help, Lord Jesus, you will help me to love my husband the way he should be loved and the way you want me to love him, in the *(continued)* *Love Him*

name of Jesus Christ. Thank you, Lord Jesus, for helping me to love my future hubby. In the name of Jesus Christ,

    Amen.

Plan Date Nights

Dear Lord Jesus,

    I pray I will plan date nights with my future hubby. I pray I will also desire to spend quality time with him out of my love for him and you, Lord Jesus. I pray you will orchestrate these date nights. I pray these date nights will bring you much glory, honor, and praise. I pray you, Lord Jesus, will be at the center of every date night. I pray we'll focus on you during the date nights. I pray our relationship with you and each other will grow during these date nights. I pray we'll have insight and revelations revealed during these date nights. I pray the date nights will help take us to the next level in you, Lord Jesus, and the next level in our marriage. I pray we'll continue to grow *(continued)*   **Plan Date Nights**

closer after the date nights, and our lives will forever be changed, all for your kingdom, glory, and purpose. I pray you will always show up and show out during our date nights with you, Lord Jesus. In the name of Jesus. Hallelujah! Thank you, Jesus! You're worthy of the praise. All glory, all honor, and all praise belong to you, Lord Jesus. Glory to your name, Lord Jesus. Thank you, Lord Jesus.

    Amen. Amen. Amen.

Tell Him You Love Him

Dear Lord Jesus,

    I pray I will tell my future hubby that I love him. I pray he will know I love him and not have to guess or wonder if I do. I pray that speaking to him will convey that I do love him. I pray he will rest in my love for him. I pray he will feel secure in my love for him. I pray he will feel confident in my love for him. I pray he never doubts my love for him. I pray my words of affirmation of my love for him will be pleasant to his ears. I pray I will love him with words, deeds, and actions. I pray there's always evidence of my love for him. I pray my love for him is unwavering and consistent in the name of Jesus Christ. Please help me to love my future hubby unconditionally. Please help me remember (continued) *Tell Him You Love Him*

to always confess my love to him because of my love for him and you, Lord Jesus. Thank you, Lord Jesus, for giving me the capacity to love my future hubby and express my love for him in the name of Jesus Christ. Thank you, Lord Jesus. In the name of Jesus Christ,

Amen.

Forgive Easily

Dear Lord Jesus,

    I pray I will forgive my future hubby easily. I pray you will make it easy for me to forgive him in the name of Jesus Christ. I pray my love will be so great for him that it is difficult to hold a grudge or unforgiveness in my heart. I pray you grace me to have a greater measure of love in my heart for my hubby that is needed to love and forgive him properly. I pray I am not easily offended by him. I pray I am not easily irritated by him. I pray I am not expecting more than he's able to give. I pray I don't place unrealistic expectations or demands on him. I pray I will treat him how I want to be treated and give him grace and mercy the way you give me grace and mercy. For blessed are the *(continued)* # Forgive Easily

merciful, for they will receive mercy. As I show mercy to my future hubby, I pray I will receive mercy in the name of Jesus Christ. Through the mercy that I show, I pray my love will grow. The more mercy I show, the more love I will have for him, and the easier it will be to forgive him. Thank you, Lord Jesus, for helping me to love my future hubby and helping me to forgive him easily. You're so awesome, Lord Jesus. You're so helpful, Lord Jesus. You're worthy to be praised. Thank you, Lord Jesus,

    Amen.

Give Grace

Dear Lord Jesus,

    I pray I will give grace to my future hubby. I pray you will help me to give grace to him. I pray I will make allowance for his faults. I pray I don't expect perfection but effort. I pray I don't place unreasonable demands on him. I pray I will be realistic with my future hubby. I pray I will always expect the best and give grace to allow the best to happen for us. Thank you, Lord, for showing me that the recipe for a successful marriage is giving grace to each other and loving each other unconditionally, regardless of faults. I pray for the grace to love each other with unmerited favor and be a blessing to each other regardless of our shortcomings and flaws. Thank you, Lord *(continued)*   *Give Grace*

Jesus, for showing me that even though we're not perfect, we can and should always give grace to each other. By giving us grace, we show love to each other, and that's how you show love to us. Thank you, Lord Jesus, for your grace. My future hubby and I may not deserve it, but thank you for it. May our future marriage exemplify your heart of love and tremendous grace for us, your people. May we always serve each other in love and an abundance of grace in the name of Jesus Christ. Thank you so much for this grace and for helping me to share your grace with my future hubby. In the name of Jesus Christ,

    Amen.

Give Space

Dear Lord Jesus,

    I pray I will give my future hubby space when he needs it. I pray I will be aware of when he needs it and provide space to him out of my love for him. I pray I will always be open to give him space so he can recuperate, refocus, and spend quiet time with you, Lord Jesus. I pray it's always a healthy space. I pray the space will be beneficial and productive for both of us to spend time focusing on you, Lord Jesus. I pray for vision, direction, understanding, revelations, and insights for where we're headed individually and where you're taking us as a couple in the name of Jesus Christ. I pray the space will be helpful in our walk with you, Lord Jesus. I pray we'll appreciate the (continued) Give Space

space, feel secure in the space, and trust the space is working out for our good. I pray we both know the space is helping us. Thank you, Lord Jesus, for the space and for helping me give my future hubby space. In the name of Jesus Christ,

    Amen.

Compassion

Dear Lord Jesus,

    I pray I will show compassion to my future hubby. I pray I will always have compassion for my future hubby. I pray I will understand him and what he's going through. I pray I will understand the challenges he faces. I pray I can relate to him and what he experiences and feels. I pray I will show compassion through the reflection of my feelings. I pray I will show compassion through reflections of meaning by relating to what he's saying, feeling, and sharing. I pray I will be the most compassionate, caring, and loving woman for him. I pray it'll be easy to show compassion for him in the humblest way, in which he feels supported, comforted, and encouraged. I pray he *(continued)*   *Compassion*

will never feel belittled but always empowered. I pray he's empowered to keep going, keep pressing, keep enduring, and keep standing through the compassion I share with him in the name of Jesus Christ. I pray I will show the same compassion you have for me to my future hubby. I pray you will help me to comfort him the way you've comforted me with loving kindness, unfailing love, patience, gentleness, quietness, and rest. Hallelujah! Thank you, Lord Jesus! All glory to your name, Lord Jesus. You're awesome and worthy to be praised, Lord Jesus. Thank you, Lord Jesus! In Jesus Christ,

    Amen.

Be Content

Dear Lord Jesus,

    I pray I will be content with my future hubby. I pray I will always be content with him and with being his wife. I pray you will help me to be content and not compare. I pray I will always appreciate my future hubby. I pray I will find ways to show my appreciation and to be grateful. I pray I will always focus on what I'm grateful for with my future hubby. I pray contentment is not based on what he does or who he is, but contentment will be based on you, Lord Jesus, and doing it all for you, Lord Jesus. I pray I will always be content in you, Lord Jesus, so that I can be content with my future hubby. I pray you will show me ways to be content with you, Lord Jesus, and ways to be *(continued)*   *Be Content*

content with my future hubby in the name of Jesus Christ. I pray my contentment will grow for you, Lord Jesus, and grow for my future hubby, in the name of Jesus Christ. Let it grow. Show me the difference between happiness and contentment, and may I always choose contentment over happiness because happiness is fleeting while contentment is long-lasting. Thank you, Lord Jesus, for contentment in my life, with my future hubby, and with you, Lord Jesus. In the name of Jesus Christ,

    Amen.

Let God Change Him

Dear Lord Jesus,

    I pray I will let you change my future hubby. I pray you will change what needs to be changed. I pray you will mold him and change him into the person you want him to be. I pray you will mold, change, and shape his character to reflect your attributes. I pray you will change his habits to reflect your nature. I pray you will change his mind to reflect your thoughts. I pray you will keep changing his heart to reflect your love. I pray you will change his attitude to reflect your perspective. I pray you will change his ways to reflect what you would do. I pray you will change him from the inside out. I pray he reflects your glory and your beauty on a whole different

(continued)

Let God Change Him

level because of his obedience, surrender, and commitment to you and his desire for holiness. I pray you will change my future hubby so his light shines brighter than ever. I pray I will never try to change my future hubby but always allow you to and pray and ask you to, Lord Jesus, in the name of Jesus Christ. Remove the desire in me to want to change him and place the desire in me to allow you to change him. In the name of Jesus,

    Amen.

Appreciate Him

Dear Lord Jesus,

    I pray I will appreciate my future hubby. I pray I will always show my appreciation to him and that he'll always feel appreciated. I pray you will show me ways to show my appreciation to him. I pray you will show me how to properly appreciate my hubby in word and deed, in the name of Jesus Christ. I pray I will appreciate him as a hubby, as a parent, as a friend, as a child of God, as your son, Lord Jesus, and as my brother in Christ. Thank you, Lord Jesus, for helping me to appreciate my hubby. In the name of Jesus Christ,

    Amen.

Listen to Him

Dear Lord Jesus,

    I pray I will listen to my future hubby. I pray I will listen to understand him. I pray I will listen with feedback. I pray I will listen with respect. I pray I will listen with my undivided attention. I pray I will listen with my heart. I pray I will listen with the help of the Holy Spirit. I pray I will listen to his words and his actions. I pray I will understand his verbal and nonverbal communication. I pray I will always seek to understand him and listen to him. I pray he knows that I listen to him, value him, value what he says, and value what he feels. I pray he always feels heard and respected. I pray I will listen to him for the betterment of our relationship. I pray you *(continued)* *Listen to Him*

will show me ways to listen to him. I pray I will implement what you show me. I pray I will always listen to hear, not just listen to respond. I pray he feels and sees your love flowing through me as I listen to him. I pray that I'll always be an effective listener and know how to respond appropriately. I pray I will show that I'm listening through my words, actions, and the changes I make. Thank you for helping me to show that I'm listening and helping me to listen to my future hubby. In the name of Jesus Christ,

    Amen.

Be patient

Dear Lord Jesus,

    I pray I will be patient with my future hubby. Please help me to be patient. Please show me different ways I can be patient. I pray I'll be patient in my expectations. I pray I will be patient in my love for him. I pray I will be patient in my desires for him. I pray I will be patient in my wants and needs from him. I pray I will be patient with his shortcomings and mishaps. I pray I will be patient with his imperfections. I pray I will be patient with his flaws. I pray I will be patient when he needs my patience. I pray I will be patient and always be patient to allow things to grow, flow, develop, prosper, and be a blessing. I pray I will be a blessing to him through *(continued)* *Be patient*

my patience for him, in the name of Jesus Christ. Thank you, Lord Jesus, for helping me to be patient with my future hubby. In Jesus' name,

    Amen.

Nice New Clothes

Dear Lord Jesus,

 I pray I will wear nice new clothes for my future hubby and myself. I pray I will care a lot about my outfits and how I show my beauty on the outside. I pray I will dress nice to feel good about myself, look good for myself, and look good for future hubby. I pray I will always look nice and dress nice with new outfits so my future hubby is always physically attracted to me. I pray I will dress modestly while showing self-love and respect for my hubby and our marriage. I pray I will buy and wear clothes that bring honor to you, Lord Jesus, and I pray my outfits won't ruin my relationship with hubby and won't hinder my witness to others. I pray I will wear clothes (continued)   # Nice New Clothes

that do not cause another believer to fall and stumble nor lead me toward temptation. I pray I'll pick out new outfits and clothing items that are pleasant to my hubby's eye and also pleasing in your sight, Lord Jesus, in the name of Jesus Christ. May everything new that I buy and wear be appropriate as a born-again Christian believer, whose been washed in the blood and is the temple where the Holy Spirit lives. My body is honored for God, all for you, Lord Jesus. May I buy and wear new clothes that compliment my relationship with my hubby and help add another level of attraction, aid towards the success of our relationship.
May my new clothes and outfits be enough for my future hubby, and may he be content and satisfied with the outfits I wear for him, myself,

(continued)

Nice New Clothes

and for you, Lord Jesus. Thank you, Lord Jesus, for helping me shop for you, hubby, and myself. Thank you for allowing me to bring much honor and respect to you. Thank you for the material blessing of money to buy new clothes. Thank you for the wisdom and conviction to know how to dress modestly and with self-respect and love for you, my hubby, and myself. Thank you, Lord Jesus. In the name of Jesus Christ,

    Amen.

Pray for Him

Dear Lord Jesus,

    I pray I will pray without ceasing for my future hubby. I pray I will pray without ceasing for his mind. I pray I will pray without ceasing for his heart. I pray I will pray without ceasing for his spirit. I pray I will pray without ceasing for his soul. I pray I will pray without ceasing for his health. I pray I will pray without ceasing for his ministry for you, Lord Jesus. I pray I will pray without ceasing for his work and job. I pray I will pray without ceasing for his purity. I pray I will pray without ceasing for his integrity. I pray I will pray without ceasing for his character. I pray I will pray without ceasing for his self-esteem. I pray I will pray without ceasing for his visions (continued)   Pray for Him

and goals to manifest according to your will for his life. I pray I will pray without ceasing for your will to be done on Earth as it is in Heaven in his life, in the name of Jesus Christ. I pray I will pray without ceasing for your purpose and plans that will come forth here on Earth, in the name of Jesus. I pray I will pray without ceasing for my future hubby's life and that with you, it will continue to honor you as Lord supreme and honor you in all ways. You will make all paths straight. I pray I will pray without ceasing that my future hubby will have all he needs to stand, endure, fight, win, and overcome in the name of Jesus Christ. I pray I will pray without ceasing for future hubby to win the battle in his mind, in the name of Jess Christ. I pray you will place a sense *(continued)*   **Pray for Him**

of urgency in me to keep praying for future hubby and to pray without ceasing for him, all for your kingdom, glory, and purpose. In the name of Jesus Christ,

    Amen.

Be Classy

Dear Lord Jesus,

    I pray I will be classy when my future hubby and I are married. I pray I will dress classy. I pray I will speak classy. I pray I will carry myself in a classy way. I pray I will be classy while showing self-respect, boundaries, standards, morals, and rules over my life. I pray I will be classy with self-love and self-care. I pray you will show me how to be classy and appealing to my future hubby in the name of Jesus Christ. I pray I will always be classy out of respect for you, Lord Jesus, him, and myself. Thank you for helping me to be a classy woman who fears God, who loves herself, and who loves God. In the name of Jesus Christ,

    Amen.

Show Him You Love Him

Dear Lord Jesus,

    I pray I will show my future hubby that I love him. I pray that I will show him I love him through my actions. I pray I will show him I love him by being willing to compromise. I pray I will show him I love him by praying for him. I pray I will show him I love and care for him by encouraging him. I pray I will show him I love him by supporting him. I pray I will show him I love him by being present and making myself available for him. I pray I will show him I love him by spending quality time with him. I pray I will show him I love him by forgiving him, letting things go, and remembering them no more. I pray I will show him I love him by giving grace to him. I pray I will show him I love him *(continued)* # Show Him You Love Him

through physical touch and physical intimacy. I pray I will show him I love him by gifts of love. I pray I will show him I love him by planning trips, vacays, outings, and date nights. I pray I will show him I love him by working together as a team. I pray I will show him I love him by telling him I love him. I pray you will help me, Lord Jesus, to show my future hubby that I love him. Thank you in advance for helping me show him that I love him. In the name of Jesus Christ,

    Amen.

Be Open

Dear Lord Jesus,

    I pray I will be open with my future hubby. I pray I will be open with him about what's bothering me and what's on my mind. I pray I will be open to my future hubby by being vulnerable. I pray I will be open by self-disclosing. I pray I will be open to new, healthy experiences with him. I pray I will be open to doing activities he enjoys doing. I pray I will be open by being willing to compromise with some important decisions that will benefit the relationship and our ministry together. I pray I will be open to necessary changes for the betterment of both of us and our future together. I pray I will be open to his likes and dislikes. I pray I will be open to learning more *(continued)*   *Be Open*

about him and truly getting to know who he is at his core. I pray I will be open to doing whatever it takes to protect our marriage and our space as a couple. I pray I will be open to doing what pleases you for our marriage and what will please my hubby, in the name of Jesus Christ. Please help me to always be open with my future hubby, Lord Jesus. And thank you in advance for allowing me to be open to him. In the name of Jesus Christ,

    Amen.

Fix My Hair to Look Nice

Dear Lord Jesus,

    I pray I will fix my hair to look nice for my future hubby and myself. I pray I will always have the desire to do my hair, take care of it, and style it in a way that is pleasing to me and style it in a way that is attractive to my future hubby. I pray I will have the finances to pay for my hair maintenance. I pray I will find time to practice self-care by treating myself to getting my hair professionally styled to please my hubby and myself. I pray these hairstyles don't define who I am but only enhance my beauty. Thank you that my inner beauty doesn't change because of a hairstyle, but the hairstyle enhances what you've already blessed me with. May my future hubby

(continued)

Fix My Hair to Look Nice

always be satisfied and content with the hairstyle I wear, and may it always be pleasing for him to see. Thank you for placing the desire in me to keep my hair done, looking nice, and professional as afforded for the betterment of my self-care and self-love. This self-care is for the betterment of my relationship with my future hubby. Thank you, Lord Jesus, for your help with this. In the name of Jesus Christ,

    Amen.

Be Positive

Dear Lord Jesus,

    I pray I will be positive with my future hubby. I pray I will always think positive thoughts about him and us. I pray I will always have a positive outlook on our relationship. I pray that he always sees me as an optimistic and positive person. I pray I will live with a positive mindset and always look for the good in life and the good in our relationship. In the name of Jesus Christ,

    Amen.

Take Care of Me

Dear Lord Jesus,

    I pray I will care for myself when I'm married to my future hubby. I pray I will take care of my hygiene and teeth. I pray I will take care of my hair and body. I pray I will take care of my face and skin. I pray I will take care of my physical health and exercise. I pray I will care for myself by eating nutritious foods, drinking healthy drinks, drinking plenty of water, and taking my vitamins consistently. I pray I will take care of myself by taking care of my mental health by journaling, meditating, praying, reading the Bible, and fellowshipping with like-minded believers. I pray I will care for myself by treating myself to staycays, shopping trips, vacays, restaurants, *(continued)*   *Take Care of Me*

and doing the things I love to do. I pray I will take care of myself by prioritizing my self-care when I'm married and not stopping it because I'm married. I pray I will always practice self-care by allowing quiet time for myself and time with friends and family. I pray I will live a balanced life so I can be my best self for me and my future hubby. Thank you, Lord Jesus, for helping me to take care of myself and to treat myself as a reward for hard work, accomplishments, and milestones reached before and during marriage. Thank you, Lord Jesus, for giving me different, new, and creative ideas to better care for myself. You're so awesome, Lord Jesus. Thank you, Jesus. In the name of Jesus Christ,

    Amen.